## 1. Introduction

Thank you for purchasing my short guide for starting up your own beauty and holistic therapy company. I have been in the industry for a number of years now, having worked mobile, in salons and my own clinic which I run from home. I also teach beauty therapy via my own company.

I can fully appreciate having had to start over three times now, due to salons I rented from being sold by their owners when the economy crashed, going from mobile to permanently based. Even from moving from one part of the country to the other. Beauty therapy is a great part time or full time role. It is what you make it. Mums use it for working around their children, and some people like me retrain wanting out of the corporate rat race to make their hobby a full time job.

This guide is not meant to be exhaustive in every aspect to consider. However, I remember how hard it was at the very beginning to get a list of items to check of the list of things to review and implement when building my first company.

Before you dive straight in, grab a pen and paper and write down the answer to this question:

Why do you want to start your own beauty therapy company?

If you can answer this in about three or four bullet points without the first answer being huge income then you are ready to move on and start planning. If your answer was based on a large income, then I strongly suggest that you actually google how much a average therapist earns!

I will not hold back punches here throughout the guide, as there is no point in sugar coating something. I love this job, I love my clients, I love feeling it gives me getting up each morning and knowing that the world is my oyster. But I do not have millions sitting in the bank. So if you think being a therapist is the key to a big income, think again and really go back to my original question.

So with that out the way, here we go!

## 2. Starting Up

Congratulations, you passed the first question and didn't chuck this guide in the trash!

Right, you got your big girl pants on? Sweet, lets start at the most logical part. Despite the tough first introduction giving those that need it a reality check, this can be one of the most rewarding career choices you make, but this is solely dependant on how much work you are willing to put in.

Its a hard slog at the beginning so remember patience is a virtue.

When trying to start a company like this it is always best to consider the following main points:

1. <u>What is the company going to be called?</u>

It seems common sense, that you need a catchy name, but you really need to make sure that you stand out from the crowd. If a name stands out and sticks with a client, you will stand more chance of them recalling it when asked by friends.

The beauty industry is huge, and it can feel quite saturated if you don't carve out your own little corner. Most people choose a company name that includes their own name, for example Beauty by Kayleigh, Nails by Kayleigh and so on. Whilst this is a logical move, it is incredibly boring, I would urge you not to go down this path. Don't be sucked in as another generic beauty company name, stand out!

My own clinic for example is based on the area of my home to which I practice from. My home clinic is based in a large conservatory over looking my beautiful garden (yes, I am proud of it, its my point of relaxation), hence the name The Sun Room. This creates a tranquil and peaceful atmosphere with plenty of natural sunlight. It fits in well with my holistic side of my company where it creates a feeling of a private clinic who puts the client at the centre of attention, no walk ins, appointment only. Their own little paradise.

So why not be creative here, have fun.

## 2. What is your Unique Selling Point?

It sounds like a sales tactic and essentially you are working in sales as part of your role as a business owner. Well, how else are you going to get clients and make a living? You have to sell the treatments you offer. A unique selling point or USP as it is also called, will help you stand out and attract clients due to a singular unique point that they are drawn to.

This is a huge part of making you the first choice for clients.
Why should a client choose you?
What makes you stand above all other therapists, salons and spas in the area?

Consider this question and jot in down in your notes, it will change and evolve so don't be afraid of scrubbing it out a few times as you figure out exactly with your USP really is. A business that is static and rigid generally will never grow it will die, so go with the flow here.

## 3. What's your ideal client?

This is a question that will have you up at all hours of the night. Don't panic you got this!

You need to figure out before you even start marketing, what kind of clientele do you want coming through your door?

Consider their age bracket, sex, employment status, location, hobbies. Everything about a client that will make them the one you want as a client. It is no use marketing to an unemployed pool of people as they will never be able to pay for a treatment. Working on someone under the age of 16 will invalidate your insurance. These are all things you need to consider.

Once this is figured out, it will go a long way in helping you create your brand, logo, marketing material and marketing content catered to the ideal client.

……

Seems like a lot to consider right even before you start? Well yes and no, but rest assured I am here to help!

Jot down ideas as they come to you, don't be afraid of keeping post it notes by the side of your bed for the 2 am ideas. Everything starts as an idea, and its how you nurture that idea and bring it to fruition that can set you apart from the general pool of therapists in your area all fighting for clients.

## 3.Home, High Street or Mobile?

You have the idea, now where for the venue?

There are mixed opinions by some as to where you should practice from, I am a firm believer in the fact that whatever suits you, is the best fit for your business. This means in essence that you do not have to fork out thousands of pounds for a commercial premises if you are working on a smaller budget, or fairly new to the industry.  There is also the options of renting a space to work from, but here is a run down of the most common venues.

<u>Opening A  High Street Salon Of Your Own.</u>

This can be the most costly of the options available. There are a range of costs to consider with this option as well. As well as commercial rent, you will ned to consider, rates, utilities, commercial property insurance, deposits, fittings costs and buying of the lease itself. This can total thousands, but the reward for this is a higher impact presence. You will benefit from walk ins, and passing traffic on the street which in turn can boost your presence.

<u>Home Salons</u>

As I have said previously, this is the venue which I have opted for. A home clinic or salon can be great for those who manage more than one business, or even have a manic family life, not to mention it is easier on the purse strings. The trade off for this though is that you never truly leave your place of work behind at the end of the day!

A home salon is where you convert a spare room, conservatory or even place a summer house on your property to work from. It is lower is set up costs, usually, and can create a smaller more intimate atmosphere for your clients. You will not have walking traffic seeing your building with this option, so you will really need to hammer out the marketing plans for this method.

Take into consideration with this method, that you will need to check with your mortgage company or landlord. It is generally easier to work this way if you own your own home as most landlords do not really like their tenants running businesses from their rental properties.

You will also need to speak to the council for your area, as they may decide to alter your council tax to include a business rates element. If this does happen do not fret! You can usually apply for zero rates due to being a small business.

## Renting a Room

For those who are starting out, renting a room can be a great way to get your face into a high street salon without the initial start up costs. A existing salon or hairdressers may rent you a room on a day basis or a percentage split. This is usually on a self employed basis. This means that you will usually be responsible for your products, equipment and marketing. That being said, there are always slight variations of this, maybe they will require you to use their own products for a slightly lower percentage that you will earn. The most standard percentage is a 60/40 split.

## Going Mobile

Hit the open road! You don't have to be tied down to one place, and can take your treatments to your clients. Remember to take in account petrol costs for the price of your treatments and set out on a map exactly how far you are willing to travel. There is no point driving for miles with no profit as a result.

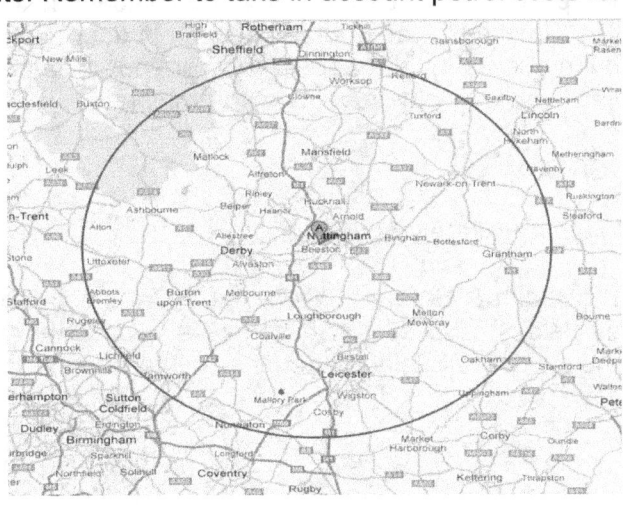

Mobile does also mean that you need to pack light, and still be able to offer a high service standard. So be smart with this option and make sure you invest in the best equipment for your budget.

Insurance for mobile services is also a key factor, you need to make sure that your car insurance covers you business travel and that all of your equipment and products are also insured against theft. The worst thing that could happen to a client is to have everything stolen from their car, that's your means of earning gone in an instant!

# 4. By-laws and Legislation

Which venue route ever you decide to go down, whether it is to run your own business or work for someone else in a salon. It is essential that you follow these guidelines with regard to health and safety, client care and client confidentiality.

By-laws

Local councils will have their own set of by-laws, these will be local laws and guidelines for businesses in their county. For example, when considering offering micro-pigmentation, or microblading you will need to apply to the council for a licence to do this at the premises you are working from. The council will direct you to their by-laws as a guide of what they require in all premises who operate offering these services. You will need to ensure that you are compliant.

Some councils will also require you to apply for a licence to offer massage therapy, or have a certain level of qualifications in order to operate within their area. So check, and double check. If in doubt you can always phone the environmental health department for your area and they will usually be able to assist you with any questions you may have.

Legislation

Health and Safety at work act 1974:

The Health & Safety at Work Act 1974 is still the main piece of legislation in this field. It applies to all people at work - employers, employees and self employed. No business is too small to escape the duties under this piece of

legislation. The act requires employers to safeguard, as far as reasonably practical, the health, safety and welfare at work of people at work. Also, both employers and self employed must have regard to health and safety of customers, visitors and others that might be affected by their activities ( or lack of them ).

Local authorities are responsible for the health and safety enforcement for the majority Beauty/Body piercing/Tattooing businesses. The officers concerned can usually be contacted through the environmental health department of your local council. They provide useful advice on all sorts of health and safety issues, particularly to those just setting up in business

The Workplace (Health, Safety and Welfare) Regulations 1992:

These regulations addresses areas such as temperature, sanitary and washing facilities, eating and changing facilities. Whilst not all aspects of this piece of legislation will apply, take stock of those that do. Not only will this keep you in good stead with legislation, but it will also cross over into the requirements from HABIA and general professional codes of ethics and practices.

Electricity at work 1989:

This ensures all portable electrical appliances are maintained regularly and that records of this maintenance are available on the premises.

Health and safety (First Aid) 1981:

Make sure your first aid kit complies with first aid regulations that must be kept on the premises at all times, and be under the control of a responsible person.

The Controlled Waste Regulations 1992:

Is a regulation to ensure all waste is collected and disposed of by a registered waste carrier in an approved incinerator.

The Management of Health and Safety at Work Regulations 1999:

To carry out and implement the findings of a work place risk assessment of the business as required by the management of Health and Safety at Work Regulations 1999.

Control of Substances Hazardous to Health (COSHH) Regulations (Recently consolidated in 2002)

Many substances that seem to be harmless can sometimes prove to be hazardous if incorrectly used or stored. The employer has to carry out a risk assessment to assess which could be a risk to health from exposure and to ensure that these are recorded; this must be carried out regularly.

Hazardous substances must be identified by symbols and handled and stored correctly.

Whenever possible high risk products should be replaced by low risk products.

An assessment must be carried out on all members of staff who may be at risk.

Personal protective equipment should be provided and staff training should be carried out if required.

Hazardous substances can enter the body via:
Eyes – contact
Nose – inhalation
Mouth – ingestion
Skin – contact/absorbed
Body – injected or via cuts
All suppliers must legally provide guidelines on how their materials should be stored and used.


Employers Liability (Compulsory Insurance) Regulations 1998:

Every employer must insure all of their employees against any injury sustained during the course of their employment.

Data Protection Act and General Data Protection Rules:

Client confidentiality must be protected at all times and the Data Protection Act/ GDPR needs to be adhered to:

You must ensure that;

- All information is stored away securely
- The information kept is accurate and relevant to the service or treatment
- That client records are available for them to view if requested.
- The client needs to agree that their data can be held, how it is used and how you can contact them.
- If you handle client data you will need to register with the Information Commissioners Office.

This new area for this legislation is quite complex and I would strongly suggest that you contact the Information Commissioners Office who will be able to discuss your needs for registering with them and going forward.

## The Personal Protective Equipment at Work Regulations 1992

Usually the requirements from this act are met if you comply with the COSHH regulations. All employers must provide suitable personal protective equipment (PPE) to all employees who may be exposed to any risk while at work.

## Disability Discrimination Act 1995 (DDA)

This act makes it unlawful to discriminate on the ground s of disability.
Under the DDA from 1996 as a provider of services, goods and facilities your work place has a duty to ensure that no clients are discriminated against on the grounds of disability.
It is unlawful because of a disability to provide a service to a lesser standard or on worse terms. Fail to make adjustments that are reasonable to the way the services are provided.
From 2004 to fail to make reasonable adjustments to the service premises physical features, in order to over come physical barriers to access.
Services can only be denied to a person who is disabled only if it is justified and other clients would be treated in the same way.

**Helpful websites:**

www.beautyguild.com - 0845 2177 384 - Insurance

www.capitalhairandbeauty.co.uk - OPI product etc

www.habia.co.uk - Code of practice for hair and beauty services.

www.businesslink.gov Will give you all the help you need in relation to legislation for both a new business and health and safety law.

................
As you can see this is not an exhaustive list, but its a starting point to give you an idea of the points which need to be considered from the moment you prepare to open to when you actually are trading.

# 5. Sanitation Sanitation

So imagine walking into a salon for the first time and realising that the place obviously hasn't been cleaned in the last few weeks? Dust on the floor, dirst on the walls, the smell of stale sweat? Makes your skin crawl doesn't it? Yep, mine too! So why on earth would you want to subject your clients to this if you could even deal with it yourself? A treatment room can get warm in the summer, so consider the smell that, that will bring with it. In the winter dirty boot prints on the floor.

A clean salon is a happy salon, and not to mention that its part of expected practices in your day to day role. Everybody thinks that being a beautician is a glamorous job, and okay, in some aspects it can be, but the majority of the time you will be cleaning and dealing with paperwork. Think about the first question that I asked you, bring yourself back down to reality.

Now here's the fundamentals. Clean sheets is a must, after every client! Yes that may mean a lot of washing for you at the end of the day, but would you want to lay on a massage couch that someone else has been laying nearly naked on? We loose skin cells constantly throughout the day as part of our body's natural functions so keep those sheets changed and clean. Wash them at 60 degrees in the washing machine to ensure that anything nasty on those towels is gone! Up side is you can claim back that washing on your taxes!

Bacteria can spread quickly and if your clients catch something which you may have missed, you will be bad mouthed from here to eternity before you even have a chance to really start.

Use disposable wherever possible. This will be slightly more expensive, but at least it gives you the peace of mind that you can just scoop everything up and pop it in the right waste bin and its basically job done apart from a wipe down. If you are busy, it saves time too.

Waste disposal is part an parcel of all this, but make sure you are disposing of your waste correctly or you could be faced with a fine from Environmental Health. Some councils require only semi-permanent make up and needles to be disposed of using a external contractor. Some are more strict and will want you to dispose of used waxing products and even massage products. Check your by-laws!

Independent contractors for removing your waste are not that expensive, and even if you are running a home salon they will still provide a suitable contract for you to dispose of that waste. They will provide you with a separate waste bin and sharps box.

Floors, walls and windows need to be wiped down with a sanitising product at the end of each day and preferably between clients as well. I would always recommend reading the labels of what ever product you are choosing as they might not always kill all bacteria. A deep clean should be conducted at least once a week. It sounds a lot, but just think of how many muddy feet are walking through, how many people are touching equipment, chairs, couches etc., the numbers can really stack up. The plus side to all this is that as soon as that client walks through your salon door and smells how clean it is their perception of your standards and professional expertise will be increased and they will know that you are competent.

If your room does not contain a sink, it is also worth considering investing in one. There is a wide range of mobile sinks available on the market, and I would strongly suggest that you ensure your chosen model provides hot water. These mobile sinks do not need to be plumbed in and usually just need a plug socket near by.

Set up your washing station, with everything you need to hand for a more clinical set up. This will do you well if you choose to be licensed in more expert areas of beauty such as microblading. It also creates a good professional image to have the ability to wash your hands before and after treatments whilst in your treatment room, your client will take note of this. Not having a sink in your room will mean that bacteria can be spread from your hands opening doors, and turning on lights in other rooms. As always think logically and think hygiene.

## 6.Products

Such a simple thing which can really make or break your business. If you choose the wrong product line and your clients don't like them, they wont be coming back any time soon.

There is an evolving market for vegan products and this is something worth considering when you are choosing your product line. I am not saying here that you must use vegan products, I am not vegan its just a point of thought! Phew right to continue....

Not only will you be using these products for treatments, but, also consider retailing them as well as a additional revenue stream.

Heavily perfumed products are something which I would personally avoid. Whilst yes, they smell lovely, more and more people are subject to allergies and you are more likely to cause a reaction with these types of products than anything naturally based.

Don't commit yourself immediately, try out a few different lines before you purchase at wholesale. There is nothing wrong with finding out what works best for you before committing long term. Remember the products that you use will also be part of your branding as a whole.

Expensive is not always best. There are many big named brands which are now selling out and advertising products for sale outside of the professional sector. Why would a client pay for treatment with you with a brand that they can purchase online or via a tv shopping channel and do at home for free? Consider thinking outside the box on this one and approaching newer brands, start up brands, or even local independent brands.

## 7. Setting up your work space

Make sure that when you choose your work space that there is room to move around your couch. It can get annoying trying to work in a tiny space where you are limited on movements. Your client will not appreciate you leaning over them to try and conduct a full massage treatment either.

Another thing to consider is lighting. If you are intending to offer lash treatments for example, then you will be able to carry out the treatment whilst not straining your eyes, remember your health is important too! The other factor with lighting is that poor lighting will result in a poor final outcome. Don't loose clients for the sake of a lamp.

There are many lighting solutions you can use to your advantage, take advantage of a room with as much natural light as possible. Secondly, consider a magnifying lamp. They are not expensive and you can then kill two birds with one stone with lighting and magnification to save your eyesight long term.

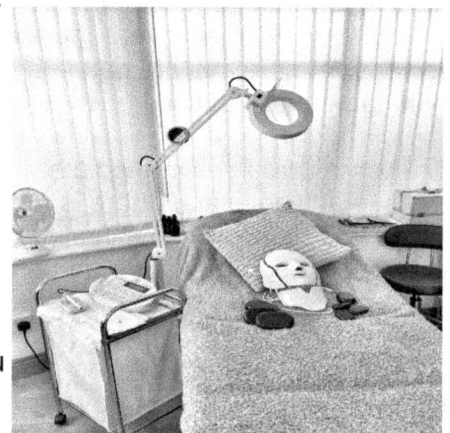

Clip station lights are also a good option for when you don't want a magnifier attached. There are many brands on the market and I will not personally endorse any particular brand, so do some research and see what works best for you within your budget.

## 8. Working Hours & Life Balance

We all live busy lives and I know how hard it is to ensure that you put the hours in building your business in conjunction with running a household. My partner works 60 hours a week night shifts, so as you can imagine I am trying to sort the house, animals and him out whilst working two jobs. Life is difficult, but you just have to find the balance that works for you.

Set your working hours to a schedule that will work within you life, and here's the secret STICK TO THEM! Do not bend the rules, because once you do the flood gates will open and you will never be able to close them. Clients will always push to see what they can away with, be it arriving late, cancelling last minute, or wanting an appointment when they know you have a day off with the family. The minute you book outside of your normal hours the client will want that appointment time again, and once you allow it you cannot undo what you have done. You would have set the precedent. It sounds harsh but its a business not a hobby. You will never get that balance without being strict with your clients.

One other point to consider is to switch your work messages off outside of work hours. I generally allow one hour before and after the day so I can catch up on messages that I have not been able to see to during the day. You will get clients messaging you at 2:00am wanting an appointment tomorrow afternoon. Again, its about setting the boundaries and being strict or you will be getting constant requests at the most unsociable hours. We all need our beauty sleep!

Don't burn out. This is a major concern when you are trying to juggle so many elements at once, family and business can be time consuming. Whilst your work will be rewarding as you are turning your dreams into reality. Remember to take time for you, even if its just one hour a week. A burnt out therapist will not provide that high standard of treatments compared to a happy healthy one. Remember to say "no" once in a while and take a little me time. Go get a massage yourself, look after the body as well as the mind.

## 9.No Shows

No Shows, are essentially where a client who was booked in with you just doesn't show up to their appointment. They wont answer your calls and sometimes will even block you on social media if you try and contact them. Now I can hear you from shouting that's so rude and I would never do that! Unfortunately it does happen, and if precautions are not taken it will end up costing you money! Think about a no show say, every month. One appointment at £30.00 over one year will cost you and your business £360.00 a year! That's further training for a new treatment, or a new piece of equipment. Think about the implications of this happening with more than one client as well!

Remember when I explained earlier that you need to be strict with your clients? This example is exactly one of the many reasons why you need to implement your rules and stick to them. Create a sign hang it in your salon, place them in terms and conditions which are sent to the client at every booking. The point is be strict. I cannot stress this enough. This is the difference between a hobby making money here and there, and a genuine income and successful business with a loyal clientele base.

There are ways in which you can enforce rules and really crack down on the no shows. When booking in a client, take a non refundable booking fee. Now here is the important point to this, do not call it a deposit. A deposit is refundable. You must call it a non refundable booking fee. I usually request 50% of the treatment costs and specify that unless this is paid and a client form completed online, their appointment request will be cancelled within 24 hours.

Also, in my terms and conditions, I specify that the client will loose their non refundable booking fee, if they fail to attend their appointment, or cancel less than 48 hours prior to their appointment.

This may seem harsh, but if a client doesn't show, you loose money, if a client cancels last minute, you lose money and you probably wont fill that slot on short notice. If you are not concerned about the profit potential of your business then you really are setting your self up to fail. Sorry I did say I wouldn't sugar coat it. If you do not make money at all and let things slide, how will you replenish expired products, broken equipment etc.?

Your time is your money!

## 10. Client Tardiness

When a client is late, it can impact the entire day, it can cause you to over run, or even not be able to complete a full treatment within the time you have remaining. Now there are two things which you can implement to help with this.

Firstly, I have adjusted the time I leave in between appointments to allow for an extra 15 minute gap. This will allow a time frame for your client to arrive up to 15 minutes late and you will not then be leaving you next client waiting.

Secondly, and this really links hand in hand with the first idea, is to implement a policy where if a client arrives more than 15 minutes late you automatically cancel their appointment and class them as a no show. Now the key to this is not to tell the client of the grace period. Try and educate them if they are late by explaining that you will try to complete the treatment within the time you have left booked for them, however, in the future in order to avoid a possible overlap into your next appointment you have booked, if your client could please make every effort to be on time. Explain that you cannot give them their full appointment time due to the fact that you cannot run into your next clients appointment. The policy will also allow you to complete a full treatment within the time you have, allowing the client to think that you have bent over backwards on this occasion to accommodate them despite that they have blatantly broken the rules.

Now this may seem a little off putting to your client at first, but if they respect you enough as a professional then they will calm down see what they have done is wrong and try and be on time in the future.

If your client chooses not come back because of being told to essentially grow up and keep to appointment times like they would with a doctors appointment, then do you really want them as a client? Because if they can walk all over you and not care once, they will surely try again!

The instant cancelling, I explained earlier is something which is pretty much a standard for most appointment based businesses. If you fail to show in your allotted time, you loose your chance and you will have to rebook. So why would you choose to be any different. Your need to educate your clients!

# 11. Example wording for Terms and Conditions.

## GENERAL TERMS AND CONDITIONS

All personal information held by XXXX is treated as private and confidential. It is used solely by XXXXX and will not be disclosed to other parties.
The client understands that the therapist may refuse to undertake treatment should this be contraindicated due to medical or other conditions that the client may present with, due to concerns regarding the health, safety and well-being of either the client or the therapist.
Each person reacts differently to treatments and in no case does XXXX guarantee any particular outcome from a treatment or series of treatments.
The client understands and agrees to pay at the time of booking the non refundable booking fee for securing their time slot. This is priced at 50% of the total treatment price with the final balance due when attending.
No refunds of any sums paid are due for services rendered or upon termination of treatment.
Therapists reserve the right to refuse or terminate treatment to any client, at her own discretion, refuse, discontinue or defer treatment. In this instance full payment is still required and no refund will be given.
Examples of when this may occur include:
If the client is under the influence of alcohol or recreational drugs at the time of treatment;
If the client has withheld or not provided information relevant to treatment;
If the client's actions, words or behaviour are inappropriate or of a sexual nature;
If the client is threatening, aggressive or violent, or in any way poses a risk to the therapist.
If the client is more than 15 minutes late to an appointment. In which case their appointment will also be automatically forfeited as well as loosing their non refundable booking fee.

## 12. Marketing

I could talk for hours about marketing, however I feel that is best placed for another time and another book. There are so many options out there for how you market to try and attract new clients. Whilst it would seem logical at first to conduct a scatter technique across the board of any avenue you can find, it would be very expensive and you will be spreading yourself way too thin. Concentrate you efforts on a couple on methods. Here are the main things to consider with marketing.

<u>Website.</u>

Now this is a must not everyone will use social media platforms, you need to be able to reach as big a audience as possible with a concentrated marketing plan. A website is also something which will make you look more professional and not just a hobbyist. There is also the benefit of SEO with a website to get you higher up on Google rankings.

There are many off the shelf template builders that you can use and these methods can save you money instead of hiring a website builder to do the job for you. SEO is not complicated to set up using this method either, there are many short guides and videos out there for free to help you get this set up.

<u>Social Media</u>

This seems to be the go to method nowadays for any start up business. Whilst on the surface there are some that make it look incredibly easy to build followers and likes, the new algorithms in place which can restrict your content reaching as many people is something which may stump those who are not used to navigating their way around it.

<u>Facebook</u>

Whilst I agree that it is easy to set up and page, post content and share to local marketing pages for free, this might not stand you in good stead long term. I admit I do still use these pages for posting offers and marketing on slow times of the year, however, the calibre of repeat clients from this method of marketing is poor. You generally get people that are only looking for the latest deal. Plus there is the fact that every therapist advertises in the same place!

<u>Instagram</u>

I am a bit take it or leave it when it comes to this platform. On one hand you get your content out there in a picture format or video in a relatively pain free way, people see your content and they like what you are putting out into the universe. The main sticking point for me is that most followers are non UK based. My businesses are not those which can be used outside of the area that I live, as they require me to be present. So how are likes and followers from other countries far away helpful?

It goes against the direct marketing tactics which are vital for a small business to grow organically. As you can see I am on the fence. Perhaps it is best that you decide for yourself on this one.

## Twitter

This platform does not have quite the same pull as it used to. For what is known as a professional business, and I am talking lawyers, accountants, estate agents and the like, this platform does still seem to fit. However for a beauty therapy business, I would personally not put too much effort into tackling this platform. I would suggest linking it to your main platform provider and just share content automatically so you have all bases covered. In the 6 years I have used Twitter, via direct content posting and the linked platform posting I have not received one client, just saying. ….

## Boosting Posts on Facebook and Instagram

Now I decided to place these together for the simple reason that Instagram is owned by Facebook. Their marketing methods are the same, the boosting of a post or promotion of your page to achieve a particular goal, say to let people know where you are based. You may see on beauty industry forums that people have declared getting adverts approved a minefield. There are things which you can do to try and limit this issue, for example do not refer to treating a condition when advertising massage treatments. Instead, I would flip the message around and state be pain free! There are self help books out there for navigating this algorithm and I strongly urge you to read up on this before you start boosting.

If you do decide to use this method of marketing, just set your budget and target market you are wanting to aim at. Remember me saying avoid using a scatter technique? Well this applies here too. You can target your boosted posts to a specific area of the country, county or town. You can also specify the age of your target audience, the gender if needed, their likes, dislikes, hobbies, employment. This enables you to target your marketing to the ideal client. Take advantage of this as you must always have the ideal client in mind.

Linked In:

This is a platform where you can write articles, post about your business growth and connect with other professionals. Now whilst this may not directly bring you new clients, you may receive referrals or even event work from this method as therapists who network well will cross refer for treatments which they do not cover.

Pinterest:

I would suggest that this is used when you are a little more established and have a solid portfolio behind you. Showcase your work on here in terms of you killer lash extensions and the like. Again like Instagram you cannot target who you are marketing to and always place a copy write stamp on your work to prevent it being stolen.

Going old school with leaflets and flyers:

I am still a fan of this method, nothing like a eye catching leaflet to get someone's attention. Now the key here is not to use constant mail shots to get these delivered. Target where you want them placed and how you get them into hands of potential clients. Stand at the school gates and hand them out to the mums when you pick your kids up from school. Leave a few in other small businesses, support local! Older clients who will be loyal and regular clients will prefer this marketing method, just refrain spamming them with information. You can also hang posters with a discount offer in your friends places of work, their staff canteens, in your local coffee shop get creative!

Word of Mouth:

This is the oldest and still the most popular form of marketing at your disposal, and best of all it is free. Provide a top quality service where the client is happy with the outcome of the treatment and feel like that they are number one on your priority list and they will tell their friends. Sweeten the deal with a referral discount, any friends they get booked in with you, its a simple concept and it can build you a loyal client base. The main word of warning here though is that mind your professional standards, one wrong word and it will be repeated.

## 13. Community engagement

Now it is entirely possible to place this under the marketing section of this guide, however, I would say that it should have its own section purely because of the importance that it can play in building your business.

Engaging with the community is a great way of using word of mouth marketing for organic growth, if you look like a good team player in the eyes of the local community then people will feel more inclined to recommend you.

Local events

If you have the opportunity to work with a local charity or fund raiser by having a stall at a local event then this can be a valuable way to increase exposure, look good in the eyes of the community and also gain new clients. Look for local well-being events, fundraisers and family fun days. Pack up a site massage chair and off you go. Offer mini massage treatments, as enticement for to the type of treatments you offer, and the level of skills which you can bring to the table.

Vouchers and money off coupons

This may sound very American, but offering £10 off a treatment as a raffle prize at school raffles and charity events can be a great way to get your name out there for very little cost. Mums will always jump at the chance for a discounted treatment, which in turn can lead to word of mouth marketing or even a friend referral booking using a further discount method. Now it may seem that you are giving away so much with discounting and free money off vouchers to begin with, however, your business may never grow if you never entice clients in from the start. Think of it as a long term game with marketing, what you loose to begin with, will be repaid with a loyal returning client base long term.

I also offer a free treatment in my clinic once a month for micro-pigmentation to alopecia sufferers. Yes this a costly treatment to offer at up to £300 a treatment, however, for me its building a connection with the local community, and off the back of it has gained an article about the business and myself in local papers as free marketing.

## 14. Free courses to take advantage of

I am only talking about a couple that I know about in the UK here so I am sorry to anyone outside of the UK for this section. Maybe it will inspire you to search out any that are available in your area of the world.

Give your clients the wow factor when they enter your premises, with more certificates up on that wall!

Barbicide

https://www.barbicide.com/education-training-barbicide/barbicide-certifications-blueco/

Skin Cancer Detection

https://masced.uk/accreditation/

Feel free to let me know of any others as you find them!

## 15. Get those certificates up on that wall!

For some reason not all therapists do this, and to be honest I am at a complete loss as to why. When a client first walks into your salon or clinic they will instinctively take a glance around the space that you are presenting as your place of business.

When a client walks into my clinic for the first time they are instantly faced with a wall of certificates and diplomas. The usual reaction to this visual point is "wow" , this is a key starting point to have with a client do you think?

If a client is impressed from the very start of their experience with you, the likelihood is that they will be relaxed and enjoy the rest of the treatment time.

You worked so hard for the qualifications be proud and share them with your clients.  Let them know that this is your business and you mean business and are a true professional with the credentials to back it up.

# 16. Professional appearance

In conjunction with the last section of this guide and the aspect of wowing your clients. Your professional appearance will also play a major factor in achieving this.

When dressing for the role can seem quite a minor thing, you could be pleasantly surprised to learn that how you dress and you hair and make up look, can have a huge impact on whether clients actually take you seriously.

Clothing:

Tunics are the most common choice in the industry, but, if you are like me and of a certain age and suffer from hot flushes, well then they are your worse nightmare!

I prefer to wear a long black dress or t shirt with my company logo on it. It looks professional but is comfortable and breathable at the same time. I usually wear jeggings with the top, so I can move easily when providing massage treatments, and the waistband is comfortable and not rigid if I am sitting for a couple of hours doing a new set of lashes. Black pumps complement this, with a added comfort insole for those long days on my feet. There are shift dresses which you can also use in the summer, just make sure what you choose is not too form fitting, you want to look professional but not too overdone, the clothing needs to work for the job you need to do.

Hair:

Your hair needs to be tied back. This is really non negotiable. If you have your hair down, it can be a health and safety hazard, especially if you are leaning over a client and working with glues or wax. The last thing you want is to end up attached to your client!

Make up:

Now this can be a touchy subject. So I will place my two pence worth here and you can make your own decisions. Make-up I feel is something which can be quite off putting to a client. A full face of make up whilst it looks spectacular and will make you feel confident, can give the client the impression that you are more concerned with your looks than with their well-being. Not to mention, it can smudge, and rub off. The last thing you want is to walk around with make up stains on your clothing. A light foundation or BB cream, with a light coat of mascara and lip balm or natural lip colour. It is better to have a healthy natural glow look than a night out on the town look.

## 17. Self employed or employed

The decision to go self employed can be very rewarding. I have to say personally, I would never work for anyone else again. The freedom of choosing your own hours, your own style of working, and your own adventure is the greatest feeling in the world.

To be self employed when you are just starting out, you will need to register as a sole trader with HMRC. This is for tax. You will be expected to submit your own self assessment tax return each year, along with paying your national insurance contributions quarterly. If you ever have any questions about the whole tax and declarations systems, then visit HMRC online, they have a vast array of guides for anyone starting out.

Being self employed does have its downsides. You will not be eligible for any sick pay if you are taken ill. So word to the wise, save for the rainy day when you need it.

The other thing to remember is if you do not work you do not get paid. There is no guarantee with a set income every month. You need to make sure that you are clued up on your finances, and prepare to cover outgoings if you have a slow month out of savings. If you get the system right from the outset, then you should have no problems should there be any bumps in the road.

If, however, you choose to go employed, there are of the benefits of sick pay, holiday pay and a pension. You are guaranteed a set income per month there is not such much riding on you making or breaking it. There is the downside however, of set working patterns, and the lack of control over the growth of the business. You will be an employee not the business owner.

Have a long think about it. Its never something that is set in stone, you can always change the direction of your career at any time. But jot down a list of what you actually want from your career.

## 18.Tax returns and accounting

As explained, in the self employed or employed section of this guide, being self employed will result in you needing to complete a tax return each year.

Keeping a good set of accounts is vital to this process being as smooth as possible. You can do this with a paper account book, and there are many made specifically for the beauty market, or a digital set of accounts. With both sets of accounts remember to back them up or make copies and store them under lock and key somewhere safe. If the worst should happen and your salon burnt down you would loose everything!

Paper accounts

Paper accounts whilst tried and tested can take up a lot of space! You need to keep receipts and account books for a while so can you imagine the space that these can take up!

Saying that there is something to be said about pencil to paper and having everything tangible in your hands. Create folders for your monthly receipts, this can be especially helpful if you are mobile for saving those fuel receipts.

Just remember to check and double check your figures when inputting them as you don't want to make a simple error.

Digital Accounts

Digital accounts can be easier for those of us who are useless with mathematics. There are systems out there that are fairly cheap in terms of monthly costs, specifically set up for those who are self employed. They will calculate your key figures to be entered into your self assessment tax return. So for those of you who are rushed for time these types of systems are a god send!

Whichever way you choose to go with your accounts, just remember to back everything up, create monthly files, and most importantly avoid letting paperwork mount up. There is a feeling of instant dread when you see a mountain of paperwork to get through in two weeks before you need to submit a return. Not only will this cause a headache for you, it will also be time which you are not working in the salon and not earning income.

One way to keep on top of your paperwork is to devote one day a week to paperwork. It will keep the mountain of paper at bay. Another aid is to create daily report sheets, these can be used to keep a total of sales, and payments jotted down so that you can just scoop up the daily reports of the week and work through those.

## Daily Report

**Week Number:**  **Day Number:**

| Date | Treatment | Amount | Subtotal |
|---|---|---|---|
|  |  |  |  |
|  |  |  |  |
|  |  |  |  |
|  |  |  |  |
|  |  |  |  |
|  |  | Total for Day |  |

## 19. Booking software or Diary

You can see a pattern forming here cant you? Old school vs new school.

Paper systems have their place, they are a cheaper option, and if the electricity went out or you had no internet service, then you will always still have access to you diary system and also to your other paper records.

This can be invaluable in those sorts of situations. I know this all to well, I had a power cut at a salon I worked at, and without client records and the booking system being on paper, I would not have been able to call explain the situation and rebook clients. This is something which can save your bacon when needed.

The main draw backs with these systems is human error and lack of automated contact with your clients.

Human error in terms of a misplaced digit of a telephone number can be terrible if emergency situations arise when you need to contact clients. There can be issues in reaching them, often resulting in bad mouthing of your business, even if it was a receptionist or another member of staff that took the details. The thing to remember is that the buck will always stop with you when it comes to handling your clients. Some automated systems will save the telephone numbers through your telephone line, enabling you to save correct phone details for clients straight away.

Lack of automated contact with your clients is another key factor that can impact on the no shows and client lateness. Booking systems often have a built in system that will send a reminder to clients prior to the cancellation period asking them to confirm their attendance to the appointment. This can be great for clients that are notoriously absent minded or bookings made months in advance.

As with everything in this guide, take away what you feel works best for you. There is no best method in terms of using paper or digital methods or record keeping, client records, accounting and diary systems.

## 20.Planning your time

When you are ready to open for business to the public, consider how you will structure your time. As you will have seen from each section of this brief guide there are many elements to consider when starting your own business.

The key to management in all things is planning. I cannot stress this enough, planning!!

Work out how to do this by using a method that works best for you. There is no hard and fast rule on managing your business.

Why not consider a planner sheet you can take down ideas, and plan your day to fit around you. Just don't be over zealous with the amount of items you expect to get done in a day, be realistic and set realistic goals.

Refrain from being hard on yourself if you don't always get everything done, life gets in the way sometimes. Just put the items to the top of the list tomorrow and start from where you left off.

When building your business, whilst it will feel like the most important thing to do is focus on the business and its growth, you need to remember to look after number one as well.

When planning your time, make sure that you leave adequate breaks in your day. Its no good having a steady stream of clients through the door if you burn out within the first three months. Eat regularly and healthily, take time out. Plan your business around you, there is no point being self employed with the benefits that come with it if you do not use them.

# 21. Pricing

Pricing is one of those grey areas. If you price too high you will have no clients. But if you price too low you will be undercutting other salons in the area which is bad etiquette and you will be attracting the wrong type of client. Then there is the issue of actually charging what you are worth. There is no point is spending thousands of pounds on training if you never make a penny of profit. Its just bad business.

You need to do research on this. Search salons in the area, search home salons in the area and try and go mid way between the two. If there is a treatment that is new to you and you don't feel fully competent don't announce it, offer a discount on it. Never allow the competition to see a weakness or they will just discount the same treatment and take your clients.

See the grey area? Business is a tricky issue when it comes to being a good profitable business, and toeing the line in terms of not being a cut throat business. The beauty industry is kind of in a league of its own. Its a flooded market, however, people do still work together if basically your not bitchy.

Don't get me wrong there are the bitches out there that will not care whose throats they cut to get to the top and win the biggest client base. But, rest assured these will have their day and the quality of their work will be tested, and eventually they will loose clients for cutting corners and slashing prices.

In the first year using the mid way method it allows you wiggle room to discount for building a client base, along with considering rising them steadily as you grow and become more experienced.

The other benefit to the middle ground, is that the penny pinchers that only visit you once unless you basically give them treatments for free, will be unlikely to cross your door. You will be just too expensive for what they want to pay.

Offer season offers and discounts to increase client traffic on slow periods. Generally summer holidays, and new year. The kids holidays generally impact the purse strings of your clients. Work this to your advantage by offering mother and daughter days.

Packages are another way of enticing clients for the right price. If the client feels that the deal is good they will buy it, sometimes more than once. Packages enable you to offer full price treatments with low cost add ons that will make a treatment look more enticing than normal. For example, when offering a massage, you could market it as a luxury massage package, a Swedish full body massage, including reflexology and body scrub. The massage and reflexology are low costing treatments to you and can easily be incorporated together to seem luxurious. The body scrub is a nice little add on that actually makes the massage process easier and in the future the client may choose this as an add on to their normal massage treatments each month.

## 22. Educating your clients and setting the ground rules.

I have discussed from the beginning of this guide that you need to set the rules with clients from the outset. The reason for this is give a client an inch and they will take a mile. Now this is not be saying all clients are the scum of the earth. I am not, its just human nature to see what you can get away with until you get told otherwise! So here is my polite rules for a happy salon:

- Please arrive on time. We will not respond to clients arriving more than five minutes before their appointment due to already being with a client and wanting to be fair to everyone.
- Arriving 15 minutes late to your appointment will be classed as a automatic no show and you will forfeit your non refundable booking fee. We cannot run late for everyone because of one client.
- Any cancellations must be notified 48 hours prior to the appointment time to allow for us to fill the appointment.
- We do not allow children in the salon.
- You may bring one friend with you to an appointment, however they must abide by the clinics and beauticians rules.
- Any complaints or dissatisfaction must be notified in writing to the clinic in a non public forum and you must allow us at least 48 hours to respond. Any decisions regarding any dissatisfaction will be final.
- No clients will be treated under the influence of alcohol or any illegal substances.
- Any decisions regarding refusing treatment is at the clinics sole discretion and is final.
- No food in the salon.
- Please refrain from using your mobile phone turn it off and relax

As you can see they are simple and concise. The easier these rules are to understand the less chance you have of someone breaking them. There are no excuses!

Some of the rules maybe questioned by clients. For example, children in the salon rule. I have this rule for a couple of reasons. One I do not have children, and call me a grinch but I just do not have the patience for them. Hats off to all you mums and mums to be that do, just some of us are not maternal at all. Secondly a child will investigate everything, so hands in hot wax will mean burns, sharp tweezers being dropped on a foot. There are various things which can happen and for your sanity and for the sake of your insurance enforce the rules.

There are other forms of education which need to be addressed with your clients. The main one to address in addition to rules, is aftercare. It is essential to ensure that your clients have a copy of aftercare instructions in their hand when they leave after a treatment. When you hand the aftercare instructions over, make sure you go through them with the client, and that they completely understand what they entail, and what contra actions could happen as a result of their chosen treatment.

This is the education part, if a client has a full set of lashes placed on, then they rub their eyes, do not wash them, or pick and tug on them, then when it all goes wrong and their lashes fall out early then they will be coming back to you and blaming you. So drum in the aftercare, the dos the don'ts. It will make sure that your client becomes educated in how to look after their lashes, and why you are telling them to do so.

## 23. Aftercare instruction examples

Here is an example of some of my after-care forms to give you the idea of what you need to educate your clients with.

### After Your Facial Session

Please note, however, the advice is not a substitute for the advice of a medical professional, but merely guidance to help you get the best from your treatment(s).

If you have any questions at all, please do not hesitate to get in touch.

- Avoid wearing make-up for at least 6 hours after a facial treatment
- Always cleanse, tone and moisturise your face; to prevent loss of moisture, protect the skin from make-up and to keep the skin soft and supple
- Always remove all traces of make-up at the end of the day
- Drink plenty of water (recommended 6-8 glasses per day)
- Do not undertake any other facial skincare treatments within 48 hours of facial
- Avoid sun-bathing for up to 12 hours
- Avoid direct heat (intense sunlight & sunbeds) and indirect heat (sauna, hot bath, shower) for 48 hours after treatment
- Do not apply perfume or perfumed products to the treated area within 48 hours
- Do not apply any other exfoliating skincare products for 72 hours after facial

Waxing Aftercare Advice

Please note: Some slight soreness, small bumps and redness are common and perfectly normal temporary reactions, particularly if this is your first waxing. These symptoms should subside over the next 24-48 hours. If you experience persistent redness or irritation, or if you have any questions, please do not hesitate to contact me on xxxxxxx.

Please take a moment to read the aftercare advice below, as it will aid in the reduction of redness or skin irritation after your waxing treatment:
Avoid heat and friction during the next 24-48 hours. This means:
* No hot baths or showers (cool to lukewarm water only).
* No saunas, hot tubs or steam treatments.
* No tanning (sunbathing, sunbeds or fake tans).
* No sport, gym work or other exercise.
* Avoid scratching or touching the treated area with unwashed hands.
* Wear clean, loose fitting clothes.

* Keep the waxed area clean.
* Avoid swimming in chlorinated pools.
* Do not apply deodorants, body sprays, powders, lotions or other products to the area,
* To soothe and protect the skin, apply an antiseptic cream to the waxed area regularly for 3 days following your treatment.
* Always wash your hands before applying any product.
* To prevent ingrown hairs, starting a few days after your appointment, gently scrub the skin 3 times a week in the bath or shower using a loofah or exfoliating mitt.
* Moisturise the area each day; this will keep the skin supple and help new hairs to grow through normally.

You may notice a small amount of regrowth after a week or two; it can take up to 4 treatments for your hair growth cycle to change to ensure the best results after a treatment.
Hair needs to be at least 1-2 cm long before it can be successfully removed by waxing; please do not shave between your appointments.
To maintain your smooth appearance, xxxxxxxxxxxxxx recommends attending a waxing appointment every 4-6 weeks.

Massage Aftercare Advice

To ensure you receive the maximum benefits from the massage treatment you have received then the following aftercare advice is recommended, thank you.
Massage movements release excess toxins from the body. This can lead to a "healing reaction" when your body goes through the process of cleansing itself by eliminating toxins. It is therefore normal to experience one or more of the following symptoms starting within the 24 hours following your massage;
* Headache
* Feeling tearful
* Increased trips to the toilet
* Excess tiredness
* Inability to settle/sleep
* Increased perspiration
* Skin break outs
* Flu like symptoms
* Dehydration

These symptoms are only temporary and should fully subside within 48 hours of your treatment.

Over the next 24 hours:
* Drink plenty of water. Water helps the body to eliminate the toxins.
* Avoid drinking alcohol, or drinks containing caffeine. These contain toxins and can dehydrate the body further.
* Avoid eating for 1 hour after the treatment. When you do eat, try to have a light meal and include fresh vegetables, salads and fruit.
* Avoid strenuous activity and allow yourself time to continue to relax.

Ongoing Care:
* Find time for regular gentle exercise.
* Find time for regular relaxation.
* Eat a healthy, balanced diet.
* Book your next treatment for 2-4 weeks time.

Please do not hesitate to contact me on xxxxxxxxxxxxxxx if you have any problems or require further advice. Thank you.

# Microblading and Micro-pigmentation Aftercare

It is very important to follow these instructions carefully!

Colour retention and proper healing can depend on your home care regimen.
Using Tattoo Aftercare Balm and keep the area moist for 7-10 days. Use a clean Q-tip and lightly massage a light coat over the area several times a day.
Eyebrows will require continued moisturising for 3 weeks.
This will help with colour retention.

To Avoid Swelling
A gel ice pack can be applied to the area. Place the ice pack in a plastic bag to avoid moisture on the pigmented area. Apply as needed a few minutes on then off.

Avoid
Any type of skin peels or products containing Retin-A and glycolic over the pigmented area
Any make-up over the pigmented area.
Hot steamy showers or long baths. Keep your face away from the shower head and apply a thick coating of Tattoo Aftercare Balm while bathing or showering.
Avoid soap, cream or lotions on the pigmented area. Wash and apply around the area.
No swimming, saunas or hot tubs for 10-14 days after the procedure.

Do Not
Pick, peel, or scratch. This could cause scarring and/or removal of colour.
Do not touch the area except for applying the Ointment provided.

Note
Colour will appear very intense and dark immediately after your procedure. The colour is sitting on top of the skin. Once the skin starts healing or flaking, the colour will fade considerably as it heals beneath the skin.
The final colour should not be considered for approximately 6-8 weeks after the final top up visit. Do not be alarmed if it appears that most of the colour is flaking off.
Some of this crusting will appear on your Q-tip- this is normal. This is the superficial colour and is part of the natural healing process.
The sun can cause fading to the pigmented area. Always wear a light coat of sun block on pigmented areas.

If you suspect any signs of infection (including abnormal redness, swelling, etc) contact your doctor ASAP

...........

Another way in which to educate your clients is through lifestyle choices. I mean if a client is coming to you for a massage every month and they are leading a very idle lifestyle then that back pain that they are having is never really going to go away. Why not try teaming up with a PT locally and create a dual action campaign promoting to your clients that if they truly want to feel the benefits of being pain free the action to which they need to take is two fold. Exercise and massage recovery.

## 24. Insurance

This section is more of a reminder than advice here. Its common sense you need insurance. If you have clients attending your premises you need to cover them in the event that they slip or injure themselves. You need to insure yourself against any claims against you that a client may bring if they are dissatisfied with a treatment outcome. Basically you need insurance!

There are some great options out there for you if you are trading in the UK, some of which entitle you to become members of the body as well. Have a look around and you will find what company suits you best.

The main three companies which I would recommend are listed below.

ABT

http://www.abtinsurance.co.uk/

The Guild of Beauty Therapists

http://www.beautyguild.com/

Salon Gold

https://www.salongold.co.uk/

## 25. So the end is near..........

Finally, I just wanted to say, that whilst I have tried to include as many hints and tips as I can I by no way guarantee that this guide is the be all and end all of all information that you will need.

I want to say thank you for bearing with the ramblings of a mad woman, and, I hope that I have at least given you food for thought in terms of starting your own business. I remember how much of a minefield it was when I first started and everything which I have included here are things which I have learnt along the way through trial and error.

I run two businesses as I said, run a busy household, and still with only an hour to spare here or there for me time, it works for me. I would never trade this experience that I have been on for anything. I wish you good luck on your journey and I sincerely hope that it is as fun as mine has been!

I will leave you with one last piece of advice. Try a business day planner. Stick it on your desk or on reception and you will be surprised what it can do to your state of mind with juggling everything.

# Daily Planner

.............../ .............../...............

| Top Three Priorities | Chores | Drink some water! |
|---|---|---|
| | | ONE |
| | | TWO |
| | | THREE |
| | | FOUR |
| | | FIVE |
| | | SIX |
| | | SEVEN |
| | | EIGHT |
| To Do | Things that can wait until tomorrow | Eat! |
| | | B |
| | | L |
| | | D |
| Appointments & Dates | Good things from today | Email / Phone |
| | | |
| | | |
| | | |
| Random | Ideas & Plans | Marketing Done |
| | | |
| | | |
| | | |
| | | |
| | | |

www.ingramcontent.com/pod-product-compliance
Lightning Source LLC
Chambersburg PA
CBHW071442220526
45469CB00004B/1630